Psychology of Trauma Through Sexual Assault

Flawless Dave

Table of Contents

Definition of Sexual Assault..9

   Legal Definitions 9

   Societal Perspectives 13

Importance of Understanding the Psychology of Trauma.17

   Impact on Individuals and Society 17

   Breaking the Silence 19

Types of Sexual Assault 25

   Acquaintance Rape 25

   Stranger Rape...27

   Drug-Facilitated Assault 30

Myths and Realities 33

   Dispelling Common Misconceptions 33

   Challenging Victim-Blaming...36

Post-Traumatic Stress Disorder (PTSD).........................41

   Symptoms and Diagnosis 41

   Treatment Approaches...45

Shame, Guilt, and Self-Blame 49

   Coping Mechanisms 49

   Overcoming Stigma..53

Impact on Relationships 57

   Trust Issues 57

   Intimacy Challenges 60

Dissociation and Coping Strategies 65

   Understanding Dissociation...65

Healthy Coping Mechanisms..............................69

Building Resilience..75

Empowerment and Self-Esteem 75

Support Systems 79

Trauma-Informed Therapy 85

Cognitive-Behavioral Therapy (CBT)...........85

Eye Movement Desensitization and Reprocessing (EMDR)..90

Dialectical Behavior Therapy (DBT) 94

Holistic Healing Approaches..............................99

Mindfulness and Meditation 99

Art and Expressive Therapies 103

The Importance of Advocacy 109

Supporting Survivors....................................109

Raising Awareness...113

Prevention Strategies 118

Education and Consent 118

Creating Safer Spaces 122

Overcoming Challenges in the Healing Process.............127

Addressing Societal Barriers 127

Promoting Long-Term Well-Being 131

Conclusion 135

Looking Ahead: A Call to Action...................135

Resources for Survivors.................................140

Share Your Thoughts...143

Part 1: Introduction

Definition of Sexual Assault

Legal Definitions
Over time, the legal definition of sexual assault has expanded to include a wider range of actions. Modern legal systems acknowledge the necessity for a broad understanding that encompasses a range of non-consensual sexual actions, having previously been limited to certain criteria.

Historical Context: Examine how sexual assault laws have evolved throughout time, from antiquated ideas to modern definitions. Highlight significant court rulings and legal turning points that have shaped our thinking today.

Statutes and regulations frequently shape the legal definitions of sexual assault. The phrasing is careful, seeking to provide legal clarity while including a variety of activities.

Statutory Components: Dissect the essential elements of legal definitions. Give definitions for concepts like incapacitation, consent, and force. Talk about the ways that legal systems handle the question of consent capability.

Degrees of Offenses: Examine how legal regimes group sexual offenses according to their seriousness. Make distinctions between different levels of sexual assault by taking into account elements including the degree of violence, the nature of the connection between the victims, and the existence of aggravating circumstances.

Notwithstanding improvements, it can still be difficult for legal definitions to keep up with societal shifts and comprehend the whole range of non-consensual behavior.

Interpretation and Ambiguity: Look at situations where legal concepts might be interpreted differently. Talk about the difficulties in dealing with the new types of sexual assault, such as the problems posed by technology and cybercrimes.

Consent Dynamics: Explore the nuances of consent in legal settings with this course on consent dynamics. Talk about affirmative consent and the difficulties of establishing non-consent in court.

Different legal systems have rather different definitions of sexual assault. It is crucial to comprehend these global viewpoints to promote advocacy and international collaboration.

Comparative Analysis: Explain how other nations define and handle sexual assault. Draw attention to the important distinctions and overlaps while highlighting the necessity of a unified worldwide strategy.

Legal standards are essential for proving responsibility, but they are also very important for giving survivors agency. Examine the role that legal frameworks play in survivor-centric justice.

Victim-Centered Approaches: Talk about programs and legislative changes that put the needs of survivors first. Stress the value of victim assistance programs and judicial actions that take trauma into account. Explore the nuances of consent in legal settings with this course on consent dynamics. Talk about affirmative consent and the difficulties of establishing non-consent in court.

Different legal systems have rather different definitions of sexual assault. It is crucial to comprehend these global viewpoints to promote advocacy and international collaboration.

Comparative Analysis: Explain how other nations define and handle sexual assault. Draw attention to the important distinctions and overlaps while highlighting the necessity of a unified worldwide strategy.

Legal standards are essential for proving responsibility, but they are also very important for giving survivors agency. Examine the role that legal frameworks play in survivor-centric justice.

Victim-Centered Approaches: Talk about programs and legislative changes that put the needs of survivors first. Stress the value of victim assistance programs and judicial actions that take trauma into account. Explore the nuances of consent in legal settings with this course on consent dynamics. Talk about affirmative consent and the difficulties of establishing non-consent in court.

Different legal systems have rather different definitions of sexual assault. It is crucial to comprehend these global viewpoints to promote advocacy and international collaboration.

Comparative Analysis: Explain how other nations define and handle sexual assault. Draw attention to the important distinctions and overlaps while highlighting the necessity of a unified worldwide strategy.

Legal standards are essential for proving responsibility, but they are also very important for giving survivors agency. Examine the role that legal frameworks play in survivor-centric justice.

Victim-Centered Approaches: Talk about programs and legislative changes that put the needs of survivors first. Stress the value of victim assistance programs and judicial actions that take trauma into account.

Societal Perspectives

The taboo surrounding sexual assault deters survivors from coming forward in many countries. Gender roles, sexuality, and victim-blaming cultural standards can intensify the pain experienced by survivors by creating a climate of shame and silence.

Intersectionality: It's critical to acknowledge the intersectionality of identities. How racial, class, gender identity, and sexual orientation interact to influence survivors' experiences must be taken into account by societal viewpoints. It is crucial to acknowledge this complexity to promote inclusion and understanding.

The way society views sexual assault is greatly influenced by the media. The way that sexual violence is portrayed in films, television shows, and news sources affects how people view its dynamics, prevalence, and consequences. These portrayals add to the collective consciousness.

Stereotypes and Myths: The media frequently spreads false information about sexual assault, including stereotypes. These falsehoods have the potential to foster victim-blaming, support damaging narratives, and erect obstacles to understanding and empathy.

Effect on Public Opinion: How sexual assault cases are portrayed in the media can have an impact on how the public feels about survivors and offenders. It is essential to comprehend the media's role in dispelling false narratives and promoting an informed and caring society.

The legal and justice systems' operations are intricately linked to societal attitudes around sexual assault. The way the judicial system handles cases, the terminology that is employed, and the verdicts of court cases all influence how the general public views sexual assault.

Reporting and Conviction Rates: Low rates of both reporting and prosecution can affect how society perceives the frequency and gravity of sexual assault. It is critical to comprehend the obstacles that survivors must overcome to pursue justice if one wants to promote empathy and legal changes.

Language and Victim-Blaming: How words are used in court can affect how society views a case. It is essential to investigate how legal language might unintentionally sustain victim-blaming or detrimental stereotypes to foster a more encouraging atmosphere for survivors.

Social views around sexual assault have been changing in the last several years, in part because of the work done by advocacy groups, activists, and survivors. To investigate how narratives are shifting and how society might become more understanding and compassionate, it is imperative to comprehend the role that activism plays.

The #MeToo movement and its effects: The campaign has been significant in shifting the discourse about sexual assault to a more prominent forum. Examining how it affects social viewpoints might help reveal whether there is room for group transformation.

Community Education and Awareness: Efforts to teach communities about healthy relationships, consent, and the effects of sexual assault have the potential to alter society's perceptions. Examining these educational initiatives aids in comprehending how awareness may result in changes in culture.

Importance of Understanding the Psychology of Trauma

Impact on Individuals and Society

Sexual assault survivors frequently face severe psychological fallout that lasts for a long time following the terrible incident. These repercussions, which include a wide range of feelings and mental reactions, intricately influence the survivor's mental health.

Post-Traumatic Stress Disorder (PTSD): The emergence of PTSD is one of the most widespread psychological effects. Hyperarousal, avoidance behaviors, intrusive memories, and nightmares become a survivor's constant companions, upsetting everyday routines and causing terror.

Anxiety and depression: Following a sexual assault, anxiety and despair are often increased. A deep sense of hopelessness and despair might result from the trauma's emotional toll and the enduring fear of damage in the future.

Sexual assault has an impact on relationships beyond the victim, undermining trust and changing the survivor's relationships with others.

Trust Issues: The basis of trust is destroyed when personal boundaries are crossed during a sexual assault. It may be difficult for survivors to trust others, which makes it tough for them to establish new connections or keep up with ones that already exist.

Challenges of Intimacy: A victim of sexual assault may have significant changes in how they relate to their own body and sexuality. Anxiety can arise from intimacy, and survivors may experience a spectrum of feelings, ranging from dread to a weakened sense of self-worth.

Sexual assault has an impact on the victim's general well-being in addition to their mental health.

Consequences for Physical Health: The trauma of sexual assault can cause physical health problems, such as gastrointestinal disorders or persistent pain. The complex relationship between physical and mental health emphasizes how sexual assault affects people as a whole.

Coping Mechanisms and Self-Harm: Survivors may turn to self-harm or actions that momentarily ease their suffering as a coping mechanism for the overwhelming feelings they are experiencing. To address the underlying reasons for these behaviors, it is important to comprehend these coping methods.

Sexual assault is not only a personal tragedy; its effects reverberate across society, adding to a larger story that demands our collective attention.

Social Stigma and Victim-Blaming: The way society handles sexual assault can make survivors' pain worse. A culture of silence and injustice may be sustained if people are discouraged from reporting instances due to stigmatization and victim-blaming attitudes.

Impact on the Economy and Productivity: Sexual assault survivors may have many life disruptions, including effects on their work, education, and general productivity. It is essential to comprehend these societal repercussions to put supportive working settings and policies into place.

Breaking the Silence

There is a widespread culture of silence about sexual assault in many nations. This silence, which is a result of social standards, stigma, and fear, feeds a cycle of concealment that prevents survivors from coming forward and asking for the help they so badly need.

Stigma and Shame: Survivors of sexual assault frequently struggle with a strong sense of shame, which is made worse by societal stigma. A culture of silence is a result of both cultural norms that tend to assign guilt to victims and the fear of being judged.

Fear of revenge: Survivors may worry about social backlash or revenge from the offenders if they come forward. Fear serves as further justification for people's unwillingness to speak up, keeping them stuck in a painful and isolating loop.

To erase the stigma associated with sexual assault, the obstacles preventing survivors from sharing their stories must be removed. To create an atmosphere where survivors feel empowered to come up, it is essential to comprehend these hurdles.

Cultural and Societal Barriers: Gender stereotypes, cultural norms, and societal expectations can all pose significant obstacles for survivors. To create an environment where survivors feel heard and valued, these deeply held ideas must be challenged.

Institutional Barriers: Workplace, legal, and educational contexts all have institutional structures that can be quite restrictive when it comes to disclosure. To remove these obstacles, survivor-centric policies and institutional flaws must be addressed.

It is our common duty to empower survivors to end the silence by tearing down the systems that enable them, elevating their voices, and fostering supportive surroundings.

Creating Safe Spaces: It is crucial to provide safe spaces—both real and virtual—where survivors may talk about their experiences without feeling judged or afraid. To provide these safe havens, community organizations, support groups, and internet platforms can be extremely important.

Enhancing Survivor Stories: Narratives have a tremendous amount of power. By sharing more survivor tales, we challenge cultural stereotypes, promote empathy, and break the taboo of silence. Advocacy campaigns and social media are two examples of platforms that facilitate the sharing of stories and can influence cultural change.

One effective way to end the silence around sexual assault is via education. Building empathy and busting myths about sexual assault requires increasing public knowledge of its frequency, effects, and social dynamics.

Enacting comprehensive sex education is essential. It should cover topics such as consent, healthy relationships, and the repercussions of sexual assault. We support a culture that values respect and communication by promoting awareness of these issues.

Public Awareness Campaigns: One effective strategy for breaking the taboo around sexual assault is to take part in campaigns that dispel myths, confront prejudices, and promote candid discussions about the issue. To successfully spread knowledge, community organizations, schools, and the media can work together.

Part 2: Understanding Sexual Assault

Types of Sexual Assault

Acquaintance Rape

Non-consensual sexual actions between people who know each other are known as acquaintance rape. Because of the pre-existing connection, there is intricacy that makes it difficult to recognize and resolve instances of coercion or lack of permission.

consent Challenges: Power dynamics, compulsion, or the use of drugs can skew the perception of mutual agreement in acquaintance rape cases, which frequently entail subtleties of permission. Because of this intricacy, the dynamics at work need to be examined in greater detail.

In many instances of acquaintance rape, the attack is carried out in part due to power disparities and coercive measures. Recognizing the subtle ways in which permission may be violated requires an understanding of these relationships.

Power Imbalances: Power dynamics may take many different forms, including age, social standing, and influence among a group of people. An environment where one side feels forced to cooperate even in the lack of passionate assent might be created by the imbalance.

Coercive Techniques: Coercive techniques, such as emotional blackmail, intimidation, or taking advantage of weaknesses, can be used in acquaintance rape. Understanding the subtle types of coercion that undermine real consent requires uncovering these strategies.

Analyzing the environment in which acquaintance rape takes place sheds light on the situational variables that support the commission of sexual assaults in social circles or romantic relationships.

Social Situations: Parties, get-togethers, and private areas are just a few of the social contexts where acquaintance rape can happen. To effectively handle the unique issues presented by each environment, it is imperative to comprehend the impact of these settings on power relations and consent.

Substance Abuse: The use of drugs or alcohol might make consent concerns more difficult to resolve. Substance abuse can cloud judgment, cause misunderstandings or misinterpretations of boundaries, and highlight the significance of giving informed, enthusiastic permission.

After acquaintance rape, victims have particular difficulties because of the betrayal of trust in a familiar relationship. It's critical to acknowledge the trauma and comprehend the recovery process.

Betrayal and Emotional Impact: Because the victim of acquaintance rape must reconcile the assault with their pre-existing connection with the offender, the assault frequently leaves them feeling deeply betrayed. The psychological effects compound the trauma that was endured.

assistance and Therapy: Recognizing the complexity of acquaintance rape survivors' experiences is essential to providing them with adequate assistance. The recovery process requires trauma-informed treatment, support networks, and resources designed specifically to address the particular difficulties associated with this type of sexual assault.

Stranger Rape

A terrible kind of sexual assault in which the victim and the attacker have never met before is known as "stranger rape." The abrupt invasion of the victim's personal space by an unidentified attacker, which tears apart the sense of protection and security, characterizes this heinous conduct.

Non-consensual sexual actions committed by an attacker the victim is unaware of are referred to as stranger rape.

Survivors must deal with the shock of an unanticipated violation since the assault was sudden and forceful, setting it apart from other types of sexual violence.

Examining the intense terror that stranger rape inspires is necessary to comprehend its dynamics. The unexpected run-in with an unidentified attacker makes the victim feel more vulnerable and disrupts their feeling of personal safety.

fear and Vulnerability: The survivor's terror is heightened by the element of surprise and their unfamiliarity with the attacker. People are frequently left in a state of shock due to the attack's suddenness, which intensifies the damage they endure.

Effect on Safety Perception: The victim's perception of safety in public places is permanently damaged by stranger rape. Fear of being harmed by strangers can disrupt everyday schedules, limiting independence and creating a constant state of alertness.

Investigations into stranger rape provide particular difficulties for the police and the legal system. The identification and capture of the attacker are made more difficult when there are no previous ties between the victim and the attacker.

Forensic Challenges: Since there is no known link in cases of stranger rape, gathering evidence may be more difficult. Finding the attacker's identity depends heavily on forensic tests and investigation methods.

Legal Implications: Court cases may be impacted by the lack of previous interpersonal dynamics. The emphasis frequently switches to tangible evidence and witness accounts, emphasizing the necessity of a thorough and methodical approach to guarantee justice for survivors.

Because the attack was sudden and severe, survivors of stranger rape have particular psychological difficulties. Comprehending the psychological fallout clarifies the complex process of recovery.

Trauma and Shock: The trauma resulting from stranger rape is heightened by its abrupt and unexpected nature. Long after the assault, survivors could have intense feelings of violation, shock, and disbelief.

Influence on Mental Well-Being: Anxiety, sadness, and post-traumatic stress disorder (PTSD) symptoms are possible psychological aftereffects. Providing survivors with trauma-informed mental health care is essential in addressing the complex effects on their overall health.

Drug-Facilitated Assault

Drug-facilitated assault, often known as date rape drug assault, is when a victim is given drugs to render them unconscious so they may be attacked sexually. By taking advantage of trust, this evil technique leaves survivors struggling to deal not just with the violation of their bodies but also with the betrayal of their sense of security.

When attackers sneak drugs into a victim's system with the express purpose of knocking them out or incapacitating them, this is known as drug-facilitated assault. This technique seeks to take advantage of a victim's weakness and lessen their capacity to object or give permission.

To comprehend drug-facilitated assault, one must acknowledge the wide variety of chemicals that offenders may use to accomplish their nefarious goals. From illegal drugs to prescribed pharmaceuticals, abusers take advantage of the strength of different narcotics to render their victims helpless.

Commonly Used Substances: Because of their sedative and amnesic properties, drugs like ketamine, GHB (gamma-hydroxybutyrate), and Rohypnol (flunitrazepam) are often linked to drug-facilitated assault.

Surreptitious Administration: Taking advantage of social situations where confidence is assumed, offenders may sneak these chemicals into victims' meals or beverages without the victims' awareness.

The subtle character of drug-facilitated attacks is one of its pernicious features. When victims awaken to the aftermath of the attack, they may not be aware that chemicals have been added to their systems and may be experiencing bewilderment and disorientation.

Delayed Awareness: These drugs' effects can leave victims with memory loss or lapses in recall, which makes it difficult for them to pinpoint the exact moment of attack.

Diminished Capacity to Permission: These medicines' paralyzing effects make it difficult to give informed permission, emphasizing the invasion of human freedom that characterizes drug-facilitated assault.

Examining drug-assisted attacks presents particular forensic difficulties. Specialized techniques are needed to determine whether drugs are present in the victim's system and to provide a precise chronology of events.

Forensic toxicology: One of the most important parts of forensic investigations is finding and examining drugs in a victim's urine or blood. However, some medicines might have a quick metabolism, making identification difficult. This highlights the need for testing as soon as possible.

Timely Reporting: Survivors are urged to report events as soon as possible since drug metabolism is a time-sensitive process. Delays in reporting might make it more difficult for the forensic team to locate and measure drugs in the victim's system.

In addition to experiencing the agony of sexual assault, victims of drug-facilitated assault also suffer from the psychological fallout from having their freedoms violated by substances they did not choose to consume.

Betrayal and Trust Issues: Survivors of drug-facilitated assault frequently face heightened feelings of betrayal as they struggle with the breach of their trust by a potential acquaintance. This betrayal may be a contributing factor to persistent trust problems.

Psychological Trauma: PTSD, anxiety, and depression symptoms are a few examples of the psychological trauma that survivors may have suffered. It is essential to comprehend the particular difficulties presented by drug-facilitated assault to deliver trauma-informed care that is successful.

Myths and Realities

Dispelling Common Misconceptions

➢ Myth: Stranger Danger - The Illusion of Safety

Debunking the Myth: While the term "stranger danger" is a well-known adage, it oversimplifies the reality of sexual assault. In truth, a significant number of assaults are perpetrated by individuals known to the survivor, challenging the notion that strangers are the primary perpetrators.

Reality: Sexual assault often occurs within existing relationships, including acquaintances, friends, or even family members. The myth of "stranger danger" can contribute to a false sense of security, diverting attention from potential threats within one's social circles.

➢ Myth: Only Women Can Be Victims

Debunking the Myth: Sexual assault is not exclusive to any gender. While the stereotype often portrays women as victims, it is crucial to recognize that individuals of all genders can experience sexual violence.

Reality: Men, non-binary individuals, and transgender individuals are also vulnerable to sexual assault. Challenging gender-based stereotypes is essential for fostering inclusivity and ensuring that support services are accessible to all survivors, regardless of gender identity.

➤ Myth: It Only Happens in Dark Alleys

Debunking the Myth: The perception that sexual assault only occurs in dark, isolated places oversimplifies the reality. In truth, sexual assault can happen in various settings, including private spaces, homes, and social gatherings.

Reality: Perpetrators exploit opportunities in a range of settings, not limited to dimly lit areas. Understanding that sexual assault can happen anywhere is crucial for promoting awareness and vigilance in diverse environments.

➤ Myth: Victims Always Fight Back

Debunking the Myth: The expectation that victims should always physically resist their assailants oversimplifies the complex nature of trauma responses. Freeze, flight, or fawn responses are common reactions to threats, and physical resistance may not always be possible.

Reality: Victims may respond to an assault by freezing, dissociating, or complying as a survival strategy. The absence of physical resistance does not diminish the validity of their experience or their right to seek support and justice.

➢ Myth: False Reporting is Common

Debunking the Myth: The belief that false reporting of sexual assault is widespread is a harmful misconception. Research consistently indicates that false reporting rates are relatively low, and the majority of survivors do not falsely accuse others.

Reality: False reporting is rare, and the prevailing challenge is underreporting due to fear, stigma, and concerns about not being believed. Focusing on supporting survivors and creating safe reporting environments is essential for addressing sexual assault.

➢ Myth: Only Violent Assaults Are Legitimate

Debunking the Myth: Perceptions that only physically violent assaults qualify as legitimate minimize the spectrum of non-consensual experiences. Sexual assault encompasses a range of behaviors that violate consent and personal boundaries.

Reality: Coercion, manipulation, and non-consensual actions that fall short of physical violence are still forms of sexual assault. Recognizing the nuances of these experiences is crucial for understanding the diverse ways in which consent can be violated.

Challenging Victim-Blaming

Victim blaming is a pervasive societal phenomenon where individuals subjected to harm, particularly sexual assault, face unwarranted blame and judgment. This blaming narrative often shifts responsibility from perpetrators to survivors, perpetuating harmful stereotypes and inhibiting justice.

Shifting Responsibility: Victim-blaming often involves placing the responsibility for the assault on the survivor rather than the perpetrator. This can manifest in questions or statements insinuating that the survivor's actions, choices, or attire somehow invited or justified the assault.

Cultural and Gender Dynamics: Victim-blaming is deeply rooted in cultural and gender dynamics, reflecting societal norms and expectations. Stereotypes around gender roles and sexuality can exacerbate victim-blaming attitudes, placing unrealistic expectations on survivors to prevent their victimization.

➢ **Myth: It's About What They Wore**

Debunking the Myth: Attire is not a precursor to sexual assault. Victim blaming often fixates on clothing choices, perpetuating the false idea that provocative attire invites assault. In reality, assault is about power and control, not clothing.

Reality: Clothing does not determine consent. The focus should shift from scrutinizing what survivors wear to addressing the root causes of sexual assault: the actions and choices of perpetrators.

> **Myth: They Were Drinking - It's Their Fault**

Debunking the Myth: Consuming alcohol or being inebriated does not excuse or justify sexual assault. Blaming survivors for their alcohol consumption perpetuates the false notion that they are responsible for the actions of perpetrators.

Reality: Consent cannot be given if someone is incapacitated by alcohol or drugs. The responsibility lies with the person who commits the assault, not the survivor's state of sobriety.

> **Myth: They Should Have Fought Back Harder**

Debunking the Myth: Expecting survivors to exhibit certain behaviors during an assault oversimplifies trauma responses. Freeze, flight, or fawn responses are common and do not invalidate the experience.

Reality: The diverse ways individuals respond to trauma should be acknowledged and respected. Lack of physical resistance does not diminish the gravity of the assault or the survivor's right to seek justice.

➢ The Impact of Victim-Blaming

Emotional Toll: Victim-blaming compounds the emotional toll on survivors. Instead of receiving support and empathy, survivors may face shame, guilt, and isolation, exacerbating the trauma.

Barriers to Reporting: Fear of judgment and victim-blaming often discourage survivors from reporting assaults. This underreporting hinders efforts to hold perpetrators accountable and perpetuates a culture of impunity.

➢ Shifting the Narrative

Educating Society: Challenging victim-blaming requires a collective effort to educate society about consent, trauma responses, and the complexities of sexual assault. Public awareness campaigns and educational programs can shift societal attitudes.

Legal Reforms: Advocacy for legal reforms that prioritize survivor-centered approaches and sensitivity to trauma is crucial. Legal systems should be designed to protect survivors and hold perpetrators accountable without perpetuating victim-blaming narratives.

Part 3: The Psychological Effects of Sexual Assault

Post-Traumatic Stress Disorder (PTSD)

Symptoms and Diagnosis

Trauma is an intricate psychological reaction to an upsetting incident or sequence of incidents. It can have a significant and enduring impact on a person's physical, mental, and emotional health.

> ➢ **Frequent Signs of Trauma:**

Recurrences and Persistent Memories

Symptoms: People may relive the horrific incident in their minds, finding it to be extremely vivid and upsetting. Numerous things have the potential to cause these memories, which may be quite distressing emotionally.

Impact: Flashbacks can cause anxiety to spike and interfere with day-to-day activities. The added emotional load is the result of not being able to control when these memories resurface.

> ➢ **Avoidance and numbness**

Symptoms: Survivors frequently take extreme measures to block off memories of the tragedy. This might entail staying away from specific locations, persons, or events-related activities. Emotional numbness and a detached feeling are also typical.

Impact: Although avoidance is a coping strategy, it might impede the process of healing. Relationships and a person's capacity to fully participate in life might be impacted by emotional numbness.

➢ Hypervigilance and Hyperarousal

Symptoms: A heightened level of alertness, marked by heightened irritability, difficulties falling asleep, and an elevated startle reaction, may be experienced by individuals. Being hypervigilant means being on guard at all times and keeping an eye out for any dangers.

Impact: Prolonged exhaustion, poor interpersonal connections, and trouble focusing can result from hyperarousal. Although at first a survival reaction, hypervigilance might wear you out and interfere with your day-to-day activities.

➢ Dysregulation of Emotions

Symptoms of emotional dysregulation include extreme mood swings, trouble controlling emotions, and erratic behavior. Survivors could experience intense emotions including dread, rage, or grief.

Impact: Emotional dysregulation can exacerbate interpersonal conflicts and heighten feelings of loneliness. Taking care of daily tasks might get difficult.

Trauma diagnosis:

> A professional evaluation

Process: Mental health specialists usually conduct a thorough assessment as part of the diagnosis process. The history, symptoms, and the effect of the trauma on the person's day-to-day functioning are taken into account.

Tools: To assist in their evaluation, clinicians might make use of standardized instruments like the DSM-5 (Diagnostic and Statistical Manual of Mental Disorders). It is important to have a comprehensive comprehension of each person's distinct experiences, though.

The criteria for diagnosing PTSD

Criteria: A particular diagnosis associated with trauma is Post-Traumatic Stress Disorder (PTSD). A person must have symptoms including reliving the event, avoidance behaviors, unfavorable changes in mood and cognition, and prolonged hyperarousal to be diagnosed with post-traumatic stress disorder (PTSD).

Clinicians evaluate the length and intensity of symptoms, taking into account how they affect the patient's capacity to go about their everyday life and their overall quality of life.

Symptoms of Psychosomatic

Relationship: Physical symptoms including headaches, stomach problems, and persistent discomfort might be indicators of trauma. The deep relationship between psychological and physical well-being is highlighted by the mind-body link.

Holistic Approach: A holistic approach to recovery requires an understanding of the bodily effects of trauma. Recovering typically requires integrated treatment that takes both physical and emotional health into account.

Sensitivity to Culture

Importance: The expression and experience of trauma are greatly influenced by cultural influences. Clinicians need to take cultural sensitivity into account while diagnosing patients, taking into account different cultural norms, belief systems, and coping techniques.

Communication: Accurate diagnosis and the creation of treatment programs that are sensitive to cultural differences depend on effective communication and collaboration with people from a variety of cultural backgrounds.

Treatment Approaches

Healing from trauma is similar to healing from a complex wound that affects the body, mind, and emotions. A comprehensive strategy that takes into account all aspects of the trauma survivor's experience is necessary for effective trauma rehabilitation.

> ➤ **Therapeutic Interventions**

Trauma-Informed Therapy

Approach: The foundation of trauma rehabilitation is trauma-informed therapy. This method's trained therapists emphasize safety, trust, and participation in the therapy interaction while acknowledging the presence and effects of trauma.

Modalities: Therapies can be customized to meet the specific requirements of trauma survivors using a variety of modalities, including Dialectical Behavior Therapy (DBT), Eye Movement Desensitization and Reprocessing (EMDR), and Cognitive Behavioral Therapy (CBT).

> ➤ **Medications as a Helping Instrument**

Psychopharmacology

role: Drugs can help people heal from trauma, especially if they also have co-occurring mental health issues including anxiety, depression, or sleep difficulties. The goals of psychopharmacology are to reduce symptoms and improve the patient's ability to participate in therapeutic activities.

Collaborative Decision-Making: A person's mental health physician and themselves work together to prescribe medicines. Informed decision-making necessitates taking into account the person's preferences, prospective advantages, and side effects.

➤ Self-Regulation and Mindfulness

Grounding Techniques

Goal: Self-regulation and mindfulness practices support survivors in controlling their intense emotions and being in the moment. Deep breathing, meditation, and sensory awareness are examples of grounding techniques that may be effective tools for reestablishing your connection to the present.

Empowerment: By giving survivors the ability to take charge of their responses, these strategies increase their feeling of self-efficacy in handling difficult emotions.

➤ Integrative Methods of Healing

Body-Centered Therapies

Connection: The body stores trauma in addition to the mind. The goal of body-centered treatments, such as yoga, dance/movement therapy, and somatic experience, is to integrate emotional and physical healing.

Release: By using body awareness exercises, breath work, and mindful movement, these methods help people let go of trauma that has been held and foster a comprehensive feeling of well-being.

> ### Creating Networks of Support

Communities and Support Groups

Validation: Sharing stories with people who comprehend and validate their emotions is made possible for survivors by joining support groups. Support from the community lessens feelings of loneliness and promotes a sense of belonging.

Empowerment: Survivors frequently find strength and empowerment from their shared experiences, which helps to build a network of support and understanding that may be helpful along the way to recovery.

> ### Treatment with Cultural Competence

Culturally Appropriate Methods

Acknowledgment: Trauma healing needs to be culturally competent, taking into account the various origins, worldviews, and coping strategies that people have. To treat patients effectively and compassionately, therapists must understand and be attentive to cultural quirks.

inclusion: Including cultural values and customs in treatment techniques guarantees inclusion and makes treatments more pertinent when considering the survivor's cultural identity.

> **Increasing Resilience**

Methods Based on Strengths

Focus: A strengths-based approach that highlights the survivor's inner qualities, coping skills, and resilience can be beneficial for trauma rehabilitation. A feeling of agency and self-efficacy is fostered when the emphasis is shifted from disease to resilience.

Empowerment: Helping survivors identify their innate talents builds a positive outlook, empowerment, and self-belief in their capacity to overcome the obstacles in their path to recovery.

Shame, Guilt, and Self-Blame

Coping Mechanisms

Coping mechanisms are techniques people employ to handle stress, get over obstacles, and deal with trauma's aftereffects. Building strong coping skills is crucial for survivors to regain control and fortitude in the face of hardship.

> ➤ **Effective Coping Techniques**

Mindfulness Practices

The goal of mindfulness practices is to develop an unjudging awareness of the current moment. Survivors can better control their overpowering emotions and regain a sense of present-moment awareness by engaging in techniques like meditation, deep breathing, and focused observation.

Benefits: Mindfulness improves general well-being, lowers anxiety, and encourages emotional regulation. It gives survivors the ability to become aware of their thoughts and feelings without passing judgment.

Setting boundaries:

Importance: Survivors must establish and uphold appropriate limits. This entails setting boundaries for oneself, speaking out when necessary, and placing self-care first.

Boundaries provide survivors the capacity to protect their physical and mental health. Defined boundaries let people feel in charge and have agency in their interactions with others.

➢ Creative Expression

Art and Writing

Outlet: Survivors can externalize their feelings and experiences by expressing themselves creatively via writing, painting, or other mediums. Processing trauma can find a potent release in artistic expression.

Remedial: Taking part in artistic endeavors offers a conduit for introspection and release. It can support the development of a sense of empowerment via self-expression and help make sense of complicated emotions.

➢ Seeking Expert Assistance

The role of therapy and counseling:

Getting professional assistance is essential for managing trauma. Therapists give support and evidence-based therapies while creating a safe environment for survivors to examine and process their experiences.

Validation: Counseling gives survivors' experiences a voice and equips them with skills to overcome obstacles. Individual requirements can be catered for in a variety of therapeutic techniques, such as Eye Movement Desensitization and Reprocessing (EMDR) and Cognitive Behavioral Therapy (CBT).

> ## ➤ Exercise and Self-Treatment

Exercise and Movement

Benefits: Research has shown a connection between better mental and physical health. Frequent exercise increases feel-good hormones, lowers stress hormones, and releases endorphins.

Empowerment: Engaging in physical activity may be a powerful coping strategy. Whether it's by doing yoga, walking, or organized exercise, survivors may take back control over their bodies.

Self-Care Practices:

Putting one's well-being first entails taking deliberate measures. This might involve doing things like getting enough sleep, eating a healthy diet, and doing enjoyable and relaxing things.

Importance: Making self-care a priority is essential for resilience and general health. It strengthens the idea that survivors should be treated with respect and care and fosters a healthy relationship with oneself.

➤ Connecting with Supportive Networks

Developing Connections:

An essential coping strategy is to establish and maintain supportive connections. Building relationships with loved ones, friends, and support groups can help fight feelings of loneliness.

Validation: Empathy, a sense of belonging, and validation are all provided via supportive networks. Talking about experiences with like-minded people may be a reassuring and motivating thing.

➤ Grounding Methods

Sensory Grounding

Definition: Grounding methods assist people in maintaining a sense of present-moment awareness. Using one's senses as a means of anchoring oneself and lowering anxiety is known as sensory grounding.

Examples of techniques include practicing mindful breathing, listening to relaxing noises, and concentrating on how something feels. These methods are particularly beneficial in stressful or anxious situations.

Overcoming Stigma

The stigma associated with trauma is a widespread social problem that makes recovery from it more difficult. Stigmatizing behaviors can spread false beliefs, instill guilt, and prevent people from getting the help they require.

➤ **Displacing Common Myths**

Myth: Shameful Silence

Dispelling the Myth: Stigma contributes to a culture of silence by enveloping trauma survivors in a mask of shame. It is imperative to break this silence to eradicate stigma and promote an atmosphere of compassion and understanding.

Myth: Dynamics of Victim-Blaming

Dispelling the Myth: Victim-blaming beliefs, which imply that survivors have some responsibility for their painful experiences, are a manifestation of stigmatizing attitudes. Dispelling this misconception requires addressing the underlying causes of trauma and transferring the blame from survivors to the offenders.

➤ **Promoting Understanding and Empathy**

Knowledge and Awareness

Role: One effective way to combat stigma is via education. A greater knowledge of the frequency, effects, and difficulties associated with trauma recovery promotes empathy and understanding throughout communities.

Community Dialogues: Questions may be raised, viewpoints can be shared, and stigmatizing attitudes can be contested in open discussions on trauma. Establishing forums for conversation fosters empathy in society and lessens the sense of loneliness felt by survivors.

➤ **Mental Health Advocacy**

Campaign Projects

Goal: Systemic stigma must be challenged through advocacy. The goals of mental health advocacy projects are to improve access to mental health resources, destigmatize language, and alter legislation.

Collaboration: When activists, survivors, and mental health professionals work together, the collective voice against stigma is amplified. Collectively, they strive to eliminate obstacles to assistance and cultivate a more empathetic community.

➤ **Establishing Safe Spaces**

Trauma-Informed Communities

Definition: Communities that are trauma-informed place a high priority on comprehending and addressing the effects of trauma on individuals. These areas are designed to foster healing and support by creating surroundings that are attentive to the needs of survivors.

Implementation: Training programs, safety-focused policies, and the development of empathetic and respectful cultures are all ways that organizations, institutions, and communities may embrace trauma-informed approaches.

➤ Propaganda Against Stigma in Mental Health

Public campaigns and the media

Goal: The media has a big influence on how the public perceives things. Media campaigns against stigma seek to dispel myths, show trauma in a realistic light, and spark dialogue that advances mutual understanding.

Positive Messaging: Changing the media's storyline entails putting less emphasis on sensationalizing pain and more on tales of resiliency, healing, and the value of strong communities.

➤ Inclusivity and Intersectionality

Acknowledging Experience Diversity

Significance: The impact of stigma varies among people according to their gender, ethnicity, sexual preference, and financial standing. Taking into account the intersectionality of stigma and tackling it guarantees inclusion in anti-stigma initiatives.

Policies that take into account a range of experiences are inclusive because they provide a space where people of all backgrounds feel supported, heard, and valued.

Impact on Relationships

Trust Issues

Trauma has a significant impact on a person's capacity for trust. Complex trust difficulties can arise from traumatic situations and affect many facets of life due to the betrayal, violation, and loss of control they entail.

Definition: Deep feelings of betrayal, whether from people, organizations, or systems, are frequently associated with trauma. The breach of trust may leave survivors with severe wounds.

Impact: The stress of betrayal may cause increased alertness, distrust, and trouble confiding in others. It affects how vulnerable a survivor sees themselves and how open they are to trust.

> **Fear of Being Re-Victimized**

Root Cause: Fear of becoming a victim again might be the cause of trust problems. Having been betrayed, survivors can fear that the cycle of vulnerability and damage will be repeated.

Coping strategies: People with trust difficulties may adopt coping strategies including emotional distancing, skepticism, or aversion to intimate connections as a way to protect themselves from possible damage.

➢ Self-trust as the Basis

Crucial Component: Self-trust is the first step in restoring trust. Survivors might struggle with self-doubt regarding their discernment, gut feelings, and capacity for self-defense. Acknowledging resilience and promoting self-compassion are necessary for building self-trust.

Therapeutic Approaches: Rebuilding self-trust can be greatly aided by therapy. Therapists assist survivors in refuting their negative self-perceptions, highlighting their talents, and creating a positive narrative about themselves.

➢ Rebuilding Relationship Trust

Important Elements: Rebuilding relationships' trust requires open and honest communication. An open discussion about limits, expectations, and anxieties lays the groundwork for mutual respect and understanding.

Consistency is essential, both in words and deeds. Rebuilding trust necessitates consistent, trustworthy behavior over time, as well as a dedication to creating a secure and encouraging connection.

➢ Understanding and Patience

Individual Process: Rebuilding trust is a process that is unique to each person and develops at their speed. The individual recovery timetable must be acknowledged and respected by survivors and those assisting.

The value of patience cannot be overstated. Early pressure to trust might increase anxiety and impede the healing process. Comprehending the viewpoint of the survivor cultivates a nurturing atmosphere.

➢ Therapeutic Interventions

Trauma-Informed Therapy: Specialized therapy methods are frequently necessary to address trust concerns. Trauma-informed therapists offer survivors a secure environment in which to discuss issues connected to trust and collaborate to create coping mechanisms.

Creating a Therapeutic Alliance: One of the most important first steps is to develop trust with a therapist. To provide a safe space, therapists use trauma-informed techniques, which help survivors progressively reestablish confidence in their therapeutic alliance.

> **The Impact on Intimacy**

Challenges: Intimate relationships can be greatly impacted by trust concerns. Deep relationships may be hampered by a fear of intimacy, vulnerability, or betrayal.

Boundaries and exploration: When resolving trust concerns, partners should communicate openly, investigate one another's comfort zones, and set firm boundaries. Patience and mutual understanding are essential.

Intimacy Challenges

Intimacy might suffer a great deal as a result of trauma. Trauma's emotional, psychological, and physical effects can result in a complicated range of issues that make it difficult to form deep connections with oneself and other people.

> **Emotional Obstacles to Intimacy**

Root Cause: People who have experienced trauma may have a profound dread of being vulnerable as a result of betrayal or violation in the past. Being afraid can lead to emotional walls that make it difficult to be vulnerable and trust other people.

Impact on closeness: The growth of emotional closeness may be impeded by a fear of being vulnerable. Those who have experienced trauma may find it difficult to open up about their deepest feelings and thoughts for fear of being judged or retraumatized.

➤ Impacts on Body-Image

Trauma may cause a person to become dissociated from their body, which makes it difficult to accept who they are physically. It's possible for survivors to feel uneasy, ashamed, or cut off from their bodies.

Healing Journey: Honoring and reestablishing a connection with one's body is essential to regaining bodily autonomy. This healing process may benefit greatly from therapeutic modalities like body-centered therapy or somatic experience.

➤ The Intrusion of Traumatic Memories

Definition: Flashbacks and triggers are intrusive memories of traumatic events that can be triggered by particular circumstances. These events might suddenly reappear in private settings.

Coping Mechanisms: Survivors and their spouses can cooperate in determining triggers and creating coping mechanisms. Developing safe language, being alert, and having open communication may all help overcome these obstacles.

➢ The Value of Open Communication

Setting Boundaries: People who have experienced trauma may be more sensitive to touch and have certain limits when it comes to intimacy, physical contact, and sharing of emotions. Setting and upholding these limits depend heavily on open and honest communication.

Consent and Empowerment: Maintaining constant communication is necessary to prioritize consent and empowerment in close partnerships. To establish an environment where both parties feel secure and respected, partners should actively listen, validate concerns, and cooperate.

➢ Developing Trust in Intimacy

Building Blocks: A strong intimate relationship is predicated on trust. Rebuilding trust may entail little actions, regular communication, and a shared dedication to fostering a secure and encouraging atmosphere.

Professional Advice: Counselors with expertise in trauma-informed treatment can offer advice on reestablishing trust and overcoming intimacy-specific difficulties. Moreover helpful in promoting understanding and connection may be couples therapy.

> **Impact on Sexual Performance**

Common Challenge: Sexual dysfunction may be influenced by trauma, which can include issues like discomfort, indifference, or trouble feeling pleasure. Intimate relationships may be greatly impacted by these problems.

Therapeutic Approaches: Consulting with medical specialists, like as counselors or sex therapists, may be very beneficial. Techniques to address particular sexual issues, education, and mindfulness exercises are examples of therapeutic approaches.

> **Supporting One Another on the Path to Recovery**

Shared Responsibilities: During the healing process, partners dealing with intimate issues following trauma have a shared obligation. Patience, sensitivity, and a dedication to comprehending one another's experiences are necessary for mutual assistance.

Couples Therapy: Couples therapy can offer a supervised and encouraging setting where partners can discuss issues, improve communication, and create plans to promote closeness and connection.

Part 4: Coping Mechanisms and Survivor Resilience

Dissociation and Coping Strategies

Understanding Dissociation

Dissociation is a multifaceted psychological phenomenon defined by a break in memories, identity, ideas, and awareness. It frequently acts as a coping strategy in the face of extreme stress, trauma, or danger.

> ➢ **Dissociative Experience Types**
> - **Depersonalization**

Description: is the state in which a person feels cut off from their own body or identity. People may feel as though they are only observers, detached from their feelings and bodily experiences and having unreal feelings.

Causes: Depersonalization may be brought on by trauma, extreme stress, or worry. It is a protective mechanism that enables people to put up a wall between themselves and upsetting events.

- **Derealization**

Description: The idea that the outside world is skewed or unreal is what defines derealization. People may have a sense of unfamiliarity, dreaminess, or surrealism in their surroundings.

Triggers: Trauma or extreme stress are common causes of derealization, much like depersonalization. It acts as a buffer against overpowering environmental stimuli, acting as a protective mechanism.

➢ Dissociative Identity Disorder (DID)

Definition When a person has two or more separate identities or personality states, it is called a Dissociative Identity Disorder. At various moments, these identities could be in charge of consciousness and conduct.

Origins: Repeated maltreatment throughout childhood is a common cause of severe trauma that leads to DID. Creating separate identities is a way to deal with terrible events by separating oneself from the experience.

➢ Contributing and Triggered Factors

Dissociation and trauma are intimately related, particularly when the trauma occurs in infancy. Abuse that is physical, psychological, or sexual can overwhelm a person's coping skills and cause dissociative processes to emerge.

Other Contributing Factors: Although trauma is the main cause, a person's sensitivity to dissociation may also be influenced by heredity, neurological conditions, and a lack of a stable bond.

➤ The Brain's Function in Dissociation

Hippocampus and Amygdala: Important for memory and emotion processing, respectively, the hippocampus and the amygdala are involved in dissociation. Trauma can affect these regions, resulting in altered emotional reactions and disjointed recollections of memories.

Cortical Involvement: There may be collateral effects on the prefrontal cortex, which controls executive processes. Integration problems between emotional and cognitive experiences may be attributed to altered connections in certain brain areas.

➤ Typical Symptoms and Signs

Memory Losses: Frequently experiencing memory lapses or having trouble recalling extended periods.

Identity Shifts: Abrupt and discernible changes in one's identity, conduct, or character.

Loss of Time: Inexplicable intervals during which a person is unable to explain their behavior or feelings.

Emotional numbness is the state of not being emotionally receptive or feeling emotionally disconnected.

➢ Grounding Methods

Goal: By assisting people in re-establishing their connection to the present, grounding techniques aim to combat the dissociative state of detachment.

Examples of successful grounding strategies include deep breathing, describing the surroundings, and concentrating on sensory sensations (touch, sight, and sound).

➢ Therapeutic Methods

Trauma-Informed Counseling: Counseling is essential for treating dissociation. Treatments for dissociation that are trauma-informed, such as Internal Family Systems (IFS) treatment, Dialectical Behavior treatment (DBT), and Eye Movement Desensitization and Reprocessing (EMDR), can be successful.

Integration of Identities: To help DID sufferers develop a coherent sense of self, treatment focuses on the integration, cooperation, and communication of identities.

> ## Confronting Misconceptions

Dispelling Myths: Dispelling myths and misunderstandings is a crucial step in eradicating the stigma attached to dissociation. It's critical to see dissociation as a coping strategy rather than a sign of weakness.

Fostering Empathy: People who are suffering dissociation require an atmosphere that is both compassionate and empathic. Campaigns for awareness and education help create a more knowledgeable and helpful community.

Healthy Coping Mechanisms

Coping mechanisms are techniques people employ to handle stress, get over obstacles, and enhance their general well-being. Using coping mechanisms that promote mental, emotional, and physical well-being is part of healthy coping.

> ## Mindful Awareness

Principle: Developing present-moment awareness without passing judgment is a key component of mindfulness. It is a technique that invites people to live completely in the now.

Benefits: Research has demonstrated that mindfulness techniques including meditation, deep breathing, and attentive observation lower stress, strengthen emotional control, and increase general well-being.

➢ Establishing Emotional Boundaries

Significance: Establishing emotional boundaries entails identifying and honoring individual boundaries throughout emotional exchanges. This entails being conscious of one's own needs, feelings, and those of others.

Empowerment: People are better able to safeguard their emotional health, communicate clearly, and cultivate stronger bonds with others when they set and uphold emotional boundaries.

➢ Nurturing Creative Expression

Creative Expression: Creating art, literature, or music are examples of creative endeavors that offer a positive means of expressing feelings and experiences.

Emotional Release: By enabling people to externalize and make meaning of complicated emotions, creative expression can be used as a therapeutic therapy to aid in emotional release and self-discovery.

➢ Counseling and Therapy

Role: Getting expert assistance is a proactive and beneficial coping strategy. Therapists offer a secure environment in which people may examine difficulties, acquire understanding, and create coping mechanisms.

Destigmatizing treatment: Accepting treatment helps to destigmatize asking for mental health assistance. It highlights how crucial it is to put emotional health first and make use of mental health specialists' knowledge.

➤ Making Exercise a Priority

Physical Advantages: Engaging in regular physical activity lowers stress hormones, releases endorphins, and lifts moods generally, among many other positive effects on mental health.

Empowerment: Physical activity creates a good relationship between physical and mental health by empowering people to actively participate in their well-being.

➤ Engaging in Self-Care

Definition: Self-care is the deliberate application of one's well-being as a top priority. It includes a range of practices, like as getting enough sleep, eating a healthy diet, and doing enjoyable and relaxing things.

Significance: Upholding general health requires putting self-care first. It highlights the need to practice self-compassion and the idea that everyone deserves to be treated with deliberate love and care.

> **Creating Networks of Support**

Community Connection: One of the most effective coping strategies is to establish and maintain supportive connections. Social support offers affirmation, inspiration, and a feeling of community.

Sharing Experiences: Establishing connections with others who share your understanding and empathy makes it possible to talk about difficulties and experiences, which lessens feelings of loneliness and promotes a sense of community.

> **SMART Objective Establishment**

SMART objectives are defined as being Specific, Measurable, Achievable, Relevant, and Time-bound. Establishing attainable and realistic goals increases motivation and fosters a sense of success.

Empowerment: Establishing goals gives people the ability to take control of their lives, divide more difficult activities into smaller, more manageable stages, and recognize little victories along the way.

> **Techniques for Reducing Stress**

Relaxation Methods: Progressive muscle relaxation, deep breathing, and guided visualization are a few strategies that work well to ease tension and encourage calm.

Daily Integration: Including relaxation techniques in everyday activities improves general health, lessens the negative effects of stress, and leads to a more focused and balanced existence.

Building Resilience

Empowerment and Self-Esteem

The dynamic process of empowerment entails acquiring the self-assurance, wisdom, and feeling of agency required to make wise decisions in life. A proactive attitude to life is fostered by the development of inner strength and resilience.

> ➤ **Self-Awareness**

Basis: The foundation of empowerment is self-awareness. Determining one's values, areas of strength, and areas for improvement offers a strong basis for deliberate action and well-informed decision-making.

Reflective Practices: Journaling and mindfulness are two examples of reflective practices that help people become more self-aware and enable self-discovery.

> ➤ **Developing Self-Worth**

Self-perception: One's total self-perception is referred to as their self-esteem. It has to do with how people view their values, talents, and contributions to society.

Positive vs. unfavorable: Building a positive self-perception is a key component of healthy self-esteem, whereas poor self-esteem is typified by a lack of confidence and unfavorable self-views.

> ## ➤ Acknowledging Your Inner Power

Resilience may be defined as the capacity to overcome hardship, adjust to new circumstances, and preserve one's feeling of well-being in the face of adversity.

Cultivating Resilience: Developing coping mechanisms, viewing setbacks as chances for development, and learning from them are all part of acknowledging and appreciating one's resilience.

> ## ➤ Establishing Boundaries

Definition: Individuals create personal boundaries to safeguard their mental, emotional, and physical health. One of the most important components of empowerment is setting and sharing boundaries.

Healthy limits: People who are empowered see the value of establishing and upholding healthy limits. This entails voicing preferences, standing up for one's demands, and saying no when necessary.

➢ **Challenging Negative Thoughts**

Recognizing Yourself-Doubt: Self-doubt appears as self-defeating ideas and opinions regarding one's value or skills. It takes empowerment to identify and confront these ideas.

Positive Affirmations: Using affirmations and positive self-talk to boost self-esteem and destroy self-doubt are effective ways to validate one's skills.

➢ **Setting Empowering Goals**

SMART goals: Setting SMART (specific, measurable, attainable, relevant, and time-bound) objectives helps to promote empowerment. Establishing goals gives you focus, inspiration, and a feeling of achievement.

Celebrating Successes: Giving credit and acknowledging little victories helps people feel more capable and gives them the confidence to take on bigger tasks.

➢ **Developing a Growth Mentality**

Mindset Shift: Rather than viewing difficulties as insurmountable roadblocks, a growth mindset views them as chances to develop and learn. It encourages adaptation, resilience, and self-belief in one's potential for growth.

Continuous Learning: People who are empowered see life as an ongoing process of growth and learning. They welcome difficulties, ask for input, and view failures as stepping stones to success in the future.

➢ Encircling Oneself with Positivity

Positive Influences: Surrounding oneself with upbeat and encouraging people might help one feel more empowered. Positive reinforcement of one's strengths, encouragement, and a sense of belonging are all facilitated by healthy relationships.

Community Involvement: Participating in groups that share one's beliefs opens doors to communication, cooperation, and mutual assistance.

➢ Practicing Self-Compassion

Definition: Self-compassion is the ability to be kind and understanding to oneself, especially while facing difficulties or failing. It is essential to self-worth and empowerment.

Resilience in Adversity: Self-aware and self-compassionate, resilient people accept that failures are a natural part of life and do not lessen their value.

Support Systems

Support systems are groups of people that help each other out emotionally, practically, and occasionally financially. They are essential for overcoming obstacles in life, building resilience, and improving general well-being.

> ### Types of Support Systems
- ### Emotional Support

The definition of emotional support is the ability to empathize with, comprehend, and validate another person's feelings. It offers a secure environment free from criticism for expressing feelings.

Sources: Emotional support may often be obtained from friends, family, mentors, and therapists. Empathic expressions, meaningful dialogues, and attentive listening all support emotional health.

- ### Role of Family Support

Basis of Assistance: Families frequently act as the primary source of assistance. Unconditional love, security, and stability may be found in the ties that unite a family.

Overcoming Obstacles: Family support may be very helpful during trying times by offering emotional support, useful help, and a feeling of community.

- **Networks of Professional Support**

Role: Expert networks of support, such as therapists and counselors, provide specific guidance through emotional and mental health difficulties.

Confidentiality: People may express their ideas and feelings without worrying about being judged when they get professional help, which fosters a therapeutic atmosphere.

- **Dynamics of Peer Support**

Mutual Understanding: Based on mutual understanding, friends and peers who have gone through similar things together may provide a special kind of support.

Shared Journeys: Developing relationships with people who have had comparable struggles fosters a helpful atmosphere for exchanging advice, coping mechanisms, and words of encouragement.

- **Internet-Based Support Groups**

Accessibility: People may interact, exchange experiences, and give help in online support networks. People from different places and backgrounds can access them.

Anonymity and Openness: People are encouraged to express themselves freely and ask for guidance without worrying about being judged because of the anonymity that comes with the internet environment.

- **Workplace Support**

Team Dynamics: A pleasant work environment is influenced by support from supervisors and coworkers in the workplace. Work satisfaction is increased via teamwork and a sense of camaraderie.

Flexible Policies: Organizations that put employee well-being first by implementing mental health programs, having a positive corporate culture, and offering flexible policies also help to create a more positive work environment.

- **The Reciprocity of Support**

Mutual aid: Mutual aid is the lifeblood of support systems. People gain from both giving and receiving help as well as from improving the lives of others.

Community Strength: A support system's ability to empower and encourage its members as a whole is what makes it so strong. A resilient community is created through shared experiences, acts of kindness, and encouragement.

Adapting Together: Flexible support networks are necessary for life transitions like job changes, relocation, or reaching major life milestones. More seamless adjustments are a result of transitional flexibility and understanding.

Honoring Achievements: To promote a feeling of mutual happiness and success, support networks are essential in honoring accomplishments and milestones.

> **Quality Over Quantity**

Importance: Creating a strong social network emphasizes the value of enduring connections rather than quantity. Sincere relationships foster a sense of community and support for one another.

Shared Values: Building connections with others who have the same beliefs, passions, and aspirations promotes a feeling of belonging and comprehension.

Part 5: Trauma-Informed Approaches to Healing

Trauma-Informed Therapy

Cognitive-Behavioral Therapy (CBT)

A popular and scientifically supported therapeutic technique, cognitive-behavioral therapy (CBT) examines the complex relationship between ideas, feelings, and behaviors. It seeks to recognize and alter harmful thought patterns and actions to promote long-lasting improvement.

> ### The Fundamentals of CBT

Recognizing Thought Patterns The process of cognitive restructuring entails recognizing and combating unfavorable thinking patterns that fuel upsetting feelings. It seeks to substitute more reasonable and realistic ideas with destructive or unreasonable ones.

Methods: Methods including cognitive reframing, analyzing the pros and cons of ideas, and spotting cognitive distortions are essential to cognitive restructuring.

➢ Behavioral Activation: Linking Thoughts and Behaviors

The behavioral component: The relationship between ideas and actions is the main emphasis of behavioral activation. It motivates people to take part in joyful or fulfilling activities, which in turn affects pleasant thoughts and feelings.

Activity Scheduling: To disrupt the cycle of avoidance and withdrawal, therapists collaborate with clients to create planned activity plans that gradually enhance positive behaviors.

➢ Recognizing Cognitive Errors

All-or-Nothing Thinking: The tendency to perceive things in stark contrast to one another, failing to see any gray areas.

Catastrophizing is the act of assuming the worst.

Personalization: Assuming undue responsibility for circumstances and placing all the blame on other forces.

Oversimplifying: Extrapolating a single unfavorable experience to every facet of existence.

> **Specifying SMART Goals**

Goals should be precise, well-defined, and targeted.

Measurable: The advancement of objectives may be measured or visually recognized.

Achievable: Objectives are reachable and reasonable.

Relevant: A person's values and objectives are in line with their goals.

Time-Bound: Objectives must be completed within a certain amount of time.

The Therapeutic Partnership: Fostering Cooperation and Trust

Essence of the Alliance: The cornerstone of an effective CBT strategy is the therapeutic alliance. It entails developing a cooperative and trustworthy therapeutic alliance between the client and the therapist.

Open Communication: Throughout the therapy process, clients should feel heard, understood, and supported. This is ensured by fostering an atmosphere of open communication in a constructive therapeutic partnership.

> **Exposure Therapy: Gradually Confronting Fears**

Exposure therapy is a behavioral strategy in which anxiety-inducing circumstances or concerns are gradually faced and overcome.

Systematic desensitization: By guiding patients through a methodical process of facing frightening circumstances, therapists enable a progressive decrease in anxiety reactions.

> **Mindfulness Integration**

To improve present-moment awareness, CBT frequently incorporates mindfulness exercises. By enabling people to see their thoughts objectively, mindfulness fosters a well-rounded viewpoint.

Mindfulness-Based Cognitive Therapy (MBCT) interrupts negative thinking processes to avoid the recurrence of depression. It combines the concepts of CBT with mindfulness.

➢ **Documenting Thoughts and Emotions**

To keep track of their negative ideas, the feelings they arouse from them, and their alternative, well-balanced ideas, clients keep thought records.

Journaling Techniques: Keeping a journal gives you a concrete way to document your progress and the insights you get from treatment. It also helps you reflect on yourself.

Eye Movement Desensitization and Reprocessing (EMDR)

A treatment strategy called Eye Movement Desensitization and Reprocessing (EMDR) aims to reduce the suffering brought on by traumatic memories. Since its creation in the late 1980s by Francine Shapiro, it has been well-known for its efficaciousness in treating a variety of traumas.

> ### ➤ The Adaptive Information Processing Model (AIP)

Memory Networks: The AIP model, which is the foundation of EMDR, suggests that traumatic experiences, in particular, can lead to the development of maladaptive memory networks. Psychological symptoms and emotional anguish are exacerbated by these networks.

Bilateral Stimulation: To activate both hemispheres of the brain, EMDR employs bilateral stimulation, which is commonly achieved by side-to-side eye movements. This procedure encourages adaptive integration by making it easier for painful memories to be reprocessed.

> ### ➤ The EMDR Therapy's Eight Phases
> - Phase 1: Planning Treatment and Taking History

Evaluation: The therapist does a thorough evaluation, learning about the client's past trauma experiences, present symptoms, and current state of health. They work together to create a treatment plan.

- Phase 2: Setup

Creating Safety: The therapist assists the client in creating a feeling of security and provides education on stress-reduction methods. Clients are taught how to control upsetting emotions by using a "safe place" or "container".

- Phases 3–6: Desensitization

Targeting Memories: The therapist assists the client in concentrating on particular memories to target while conducting bilateral stimulation at the same time. The goal of this stage is to lessen the emotional impact that comes with painful memories.

Processing and Integration: As a result of reprocessing negative beliefs and integrating more adaptive beliefs, the client's emotional suffering decreases as they work through the memories.

- Phase 7: Installation

Positive Cognition: The therapist works with the client to create and implement affirmations or positive beliefs to balance out the negative ideas brought on by the traumatic experiences.

- Phase 8: Body Scan

Evaluating bodily Sensations: The client and the therapist discuss any lingering bodily strain or feelings connected to the recalled experiences. When necessary, bilateral stimulation is used to encourage further processing.

- Phases 9–12: Reassessment and Closure

Grounding strategies: After each session, the therapist helps the client apply grounding strategies to make sure they feel steady and in control.

Reevaluation: The therapist assesses the patient's development again in later sessions and deals with any unresolved pain or related memories.

> **Techniques for Bilateral Stimulation**
- Eye Movements

Guided Eye movements: The most popular type of bilateral stimulation is seeing a visual stimulus or the therapist's hand motions as they move from side to side.

- Auditory and Tactile Stimulation

Tappers and Buzzers: Handheld devices that provide bilateral tactile or auditory stimulation, such as tappers, or aural stimuli, such as buzzers, can be used as substitutes for eye movements.

➢ EMDR for Different Kinds of Trauma

- Distinct Traumas and PTSD

Effective for PTSD: EMDR is a recognized treatment for post-traumatic stress disorder (PTSD), especially when dealing with isolated traumatic experiences.

- Complex and Developmental Traumas

Managing Complexity: EMDR has been modified to manage complex trauma, which includes developmental trauma brought on by enduringly bad childhood events.

Neurobiological Alterations and EMDR: Effects on Brain Function

Neuroplasticity: It is believed that EMDR facilitates alterations in brain circuits linked to traumatic memories by encouraging neuroplasticity.

Integration of Traumatic Memories: EMDR facilitates the integration of traumatic memories into a person's larger life story during the reprocessing phases.

➢ Research and Efficacy

Research Findings: The effectiveness of EMDR in decreasing trauma-related symptoms has been demonstrated by several studies, with results that are on par with those of conventional cognitive-behavioral therapy.

> **Ensuring Ethical Practice**

Informed Consent: When employing EMDR, therapists make sure their clients are aware of the therapy procedure, possible results, and their right to agree or refuse it.

Cultural competency: EMDR practitioners place a high value on cultural competency, acknowledging and honoring a range of cultural experiences and viewpoints.

Dialectical Behavior Therapy (DBT)

Dr. Marsha M. Linehan created dialectical behavior therapy, or DBT, as a therapeutic technique. DBT was first developed to treat people with borderline personality disorder (BPD) and persistent suicidal thoughts. Since then, it has developed into a flexible approach to treating a wide range of emotional and behavioral issues.

> **The Philosophical Dialectic: Harmonizing Change and Acceptance**

Dialectics: DBT is based on the idea of dialectics, which emphasizes the fusion of notions that at first glance appear incompatible. The treatment encourages striking a balance between the demand for change and accepting oneself.

Validation and Change: Clients are urged to cultivate change for a more fulfilled life while also receiving validation for their existing experiences and habits.

➤ **The DBT Four Modules**

- Mindfulness Skills

Present-Moment Awareness: Developing present-moment awareness without passing judgment is a key component of mindfulness in DBT. Clients get the ability to notice their feelings and thoughts without being overwhelmed.

Exercises for Mindfulness: The development of mindfulness abilities revolves around methods like attentive breathing, detached thinking observation, and regular mindfulness exercises.

- Distress Tolerance Skills

Handling Stress: People with distress tolerance abilities can handle stressful situations without acting out. Distraction, self-soothing, and radical acceptance are among the strategies.

Accepting truth: Whether it is challenging or painful, radical acceptance is recognizing and embracing truth without passing judgment.

- Emotional Control Capabilities

Comprehending and Controlling Emotions: The ability to regulate emotions allows people to recognize and efficiently handle strong feelings. The development of good emotional experiences, contrary actions, and emotional labeling are some of the techniques.

Being Aware of Emotions: Including emotion control and mindfulness stresses being aware of emotions without becoming overcome by them.

- Skills for Interpersonal Effectiveness

Interpersonal effectiveness abilities are centered on enhancing relationships and communication. The skills of asserting demands, setting limits, and resolving interpersonal disputes are taught to clients.

DEAR MAN: To facilitate assertive communication, the acronym DEAR MAN (Describe, Express, Assert, Reinforce, Stay Mindful, Appear Confident, Negotiate) is used in interpersonal success.

> **The Therapeutic Relationship in DBT**

Balancing Change and Acceptance in Therapy: DBT therapists help clients by striking a balance between change and acceptance as they go through the dialectical problem.

They support advancement while validating the experiences of their clientele.

Collaborative Approach: DBT therapy relationships are honest and cooperative. Together, therapists and clients establish goals for therapy, go about tactics, and resolve obstacles.

> ### Behavioral Chain Analysis: Targeting of Problematic Behaviors

Recognizing Patterns in Behavior: One technique for breaking down and comprehending the series of events that lead to harmful behaviors is behavioral chain analysis. Clients and therapists cooperatively investigate triggers, ideas, emotions, and behaviors.

Creating Alternatives: Utilizing research, clients acquire knowledge of potential reactions and coping mechanisms for comparable circumstances in the future.

> ### Utilizing DBT: Going Beyond Borderline Personality Disorder

DBT's Versatility: Although DBT was first created to treat borderline personality disorder (BPD), it has also shown promise in treating eating disorders, mood disorders, drug use disorders, and post-traumatic stress disorder (PTSD).

Adaptations for Various Settings: DBT is applicable in a variety of therapeutic contexts and has been modified for use in group therapy, individual therapy, and intensive outpatient programs.

➢ Group-Based Learning

Organized Curriculum: Mindfulness, distress tolerance, emotion regulation, and interpersonal effectiveness are all covered in the organized curriculum that DBT skills training groups adhere to.

Peer Support: Group environments offer chances for skill practice, mutual experiences, and peer support, which promotes a feeling of understanding and community.

➢ Measurement of Outcomes

Objective Assessment: DBT uses outcome measures to assess therapy's efficacy objectively. The tracking of behavioral modifications, emotional control, and general well-being is done.

Holistic Healing Approaches

Mindfulness and Meditation

Cultivating present-moment awareness while maintaining an accepting and nonjudgmental mindset is known as mindfulness. It entails cultivating a strong connection with the present experience by paying attention to ideas, feelings, sensations, and the surroundings.

> ### ➤ The Essence of Mindfulness

Being Fully Present: Mindfulness places a strong emphasis on the value of living in the present moment, unencumbered by worries or distractions.

Sensory Engagement: Whether it's the flavor of food, the warmth of the sun, or the feeling of breath, practitioners use all of their senses to fully appreciate the richness of each moment.

> ### ➤ Psychological Well-Being

Stress Reduction: Research has demonstrated that mindfulness exercises can lower stress by encouraging a non-reactive awareness of stressors and strengthening coping skills.

Emotional Regulation: Mindfulness enables people to recognize and control their feelings, which promotes a composed and sympathetic reaction to trying circumstances.

➤ Understanding Meditation

Centering the Mind: Meditation is a concentrated technique that entails focusing attention within, frequently through mantra repetition, breath awareness, or imagery.

Cultivating Presence: People may improve their awareness in daily life by teaching their thoughts to stay present via frequent meditation.

➤ Types of Meditation

- Meditation Techniques

Breath Awareness: Mindfulness meditation frequently starts with concentrated attention to the breath. By paying attention to every breath in and out, practitioners ground themselves in the here and now.

Body Scan: This technique cultivates awareness of bodily sensations by methodically focusing attention on various body areas.

- Loving-Kindness Meditation

Developing Compassion: In loving-kindness meditation, one sends good thoughts and intentions to both oneself and other people. It cultivates feelings of kindness, love, and compassion.

Mantras and Affirmations: Individuals who use them repeat sentences like "May I be happy, may I be healthy" or send forth similar thoughts and wishes to other people.

➢ Applications of Mindfulness in Everyday Life

Savoring every mouthful, focusing on aromas and sensations, and being completely present during meals are all components of mindful eating.

Walking meditation: By focusing on each step, the feeling of movement, and the surroundings, practitioners infuse mindfulness into walking.

➢ Developing a Mindfulness Routine: Creating Uniformity

Start Small: Novices can begin with brief sessions and progressively extend them as they get more comfortable with the technique.

Regular pattern: Establishing a regular pattern for mindfulness practice involves designating a set time each day.

➢ Using Technology

Accessible Tools: Mindfulness applications offer daily reminders, breathing exercises, and guided meditations, making the practice available to people with a variety of schedules.

Online Communities: These are online groups that bring together practitioners and provide information, support, and experiences from others.

➢ Techniques for Reducing Stress

Focused Breathing: By inducing the body's relaxation response, a few deliberate, deep breaths can help release tension during stressful situations.

Mindful Pause: Including quick mindfulness pauses in one's daily routine enables people to regroup and confront obstacles more clearly.

> **Neurological Effects**

Brain Changes: Studies show that mindfulness training can alter the structure of the brain, especially in regions related to self-awareness, emotional control, and attention.

Stress Hormone Regulation: Studies have shown that mindfulness lowers stress hormone levels, which benefits general well-being.

Art and Expressive Therapies

A variety of creative modalities, such as visual arts, music, dance, theater, and writing, are included in art and expressive therapies. These therapy modalities use artistic expression as a means of promoting self-awareness, emotional recovery, and personal development.

> **Unlocking Non-Verbal Expression: The Healing Power of Art**

Beyond Words: Through art, people may communicate ideas, emotions, and experiences that would be difficult to convey orally in a novel way.

Symbolic Language: People may express complicated feelings and stories via the use of artistic creations, which frequently act as symbolic representations.

> **Visual Arts Psychotherapy**
- Drawing and Painting

Creative inquiry: The canvas for creative inquiry is provided by painting and sketching. Clients can express their inner world via the use of colors, forms, and textures.

Metaphor and Imagery: To learn more about a client's subconscious processes, therapists frequently investigate the metaphors and imagery found in artwork.

- Collage and Sculpture

Tactile Expression: Hands-on, tactile expression is a feature of collage and sculpture. Clients can explore their feelings through several senses when working with various materials.

Transformation and Integration: Mirroring the client's experience in treatment, the shaping and assembly process of materials represents transformation and integration.

> **Music therapy**

Emotional resonance: To elicit and explore emotions, music therapy makes use of sound's emotional resonance. Voice, rhythm, and instruments all become means of expressing oneself.

Customers have the option to participate in musical improvisation or composition, which enables them to craft unique representations of their feelings and experiences.

➤ Movement Therapy and Dancing

Body as Canvas: The body is used as a medium for expression in dance and movement therapy. Clients use movement as a language to express their feelings and narratives.

Promoting somatic awareness, or developing a deeper knowledge of oneself by connecting with one's physical feelings and movements, is a key component of the therapeutic process.

➤ Theatrical Investigation

Drama therapy includes role-playing and storytelling in which clients act out stories or characters that relate to their experiences.

Empowerment and Catharsis: Taking on various roles gives clients the ability to examine and reinterpret their own stories while also serving as a cathartic release.

> **Literary Composition**

Journaling and Reflection: As a way of expressing oneself, writing and poetry therapy clients are encouraged to journal, write reflectively, or compose poems.

Metaphors and narratives are used by clients to communicate personal experiences, which helps them develop a better understanding of their feelings and viewpoints.

> **Integrating Expressive Therapies**

Holistic Integration: A lot of therapists use multimodal techniques, fusing many expressive modalities to allow clients a variety of individualized exploration paths.

Individualized Treatment Plans: To ensure a customized and successful approach, therapists create treatment plans based on the client's preferences, strengths, and therapeutic objectives.

> **Using Expressive Therapies in Different Contexts**

Individual and Group contexts: Expressive therapies may be used in a variety of contexts, including community outreach initiatives, group seminars, and individual treatment sessions.

Community Engagement: Art and expressive therapies are not limited to clinical settings; they are also employed in schools, organizations, and community projects that promote mental health and well-being.

➢ Creating Healing Narratives

Collaborative Exploration: As part of the therapeutic process, the client and therapist jointly explore, co-writing tales of recovery and change.

Empowerment via Creation: By actively participating in their therapy process and developing a feeling of agency, clients get empowerment via the act of creation.

Part 6: Advocacy and Prevention

The Importance of Advocacy

Supporting Survivors

➤ Comprehending Trauma and Survivorship

Events that are too much for a person to handle are referred to as trauma, and they frequently have long-lasting emotional and psychological repercussions. Navigating life after trauma, including the path toward recovery and resilience, is the essence of survival.

➤ Fostering Trust

Trust as a Foundation: Encouraging survivors requires establishing trust. Establishing a safe environment requires empathetic behavior, attentive listening, and a dedication to privacy.

Non-Judgmental Environment: Survivors want reassurance that others will empathize with and understand their experiences, creating a judgment-free environment.

➢ Effective Communication

Validation through Listening: Active listening means providing survivors with your whole attention, acknowledging their experiences, and letting them express their emotions without any interruptions.

Reflective Reactions: Giving thoughtful responses helps people feel validated by reassuring them that their remarks are heard and understood.

➢ Recognizing the Effect

Education on Trauma Reactions: Psychoeducation normalizes emotions and lessens self-blame by assisting survivors in understanding the effects of trauma on the brain and emotional control.

Dispelling Frequently Held Myths: Dispelling myths and misunderstandings around trauma enables survivors to realize that their feelings are typical reactions to unusual occurrences.

➢ Autonomy in Decision-Making

Honoring Survivor Choices: Part of empowerment is honoring survivors' freedom to make their own decisions. Giving individuals options and authority over their recovery process promotes their sense of agency.

Making Informed Decisions: By giving survivors access to knowledge, they may make well-informed decisions on their therapy path, which helps them feel empowered and supported.

➤ Holistic Approach

Understanding Triggers: Identifying and comprehending possible stressors for survivors enables the development of preventative measures to control emotional reactions.

Creating a Collaborative Plan: A trauma-sensitive and comprehensive approach to recovery is ensured when a care plan is collaboratively developed, taking into account the specific requirements of the survivor.

➤ Strengths-Based Approach

Identifying Resilience: It's critical to acknowledge the resilience and strengths of survivors. By concentrating on their strengths, they can develop coping mechanisms and a positive outlook.

Developing Coping Skills: By helping survivors develop and hone their coping mechanisms, we provide them with the tools they need to deal with obstacles and stresses.

➢ Addressing Secondary Trauma

Comprehending Adjunctive Trauma: Supporting caregivers for survivors who could suffer from secondary trauma. To address their well-being, it is imperative to provide resources, supervision, and practices for self-care.

Preventing Burnout: Promoting self-care behaviors enables caregivers to sustain their mental health and long-term efficacy in providing support to survivors.

➢ Establishing a Connection with Support Systems

Connecting with Available Resources: Making connections between survivors and networks, support groups, and community resources guarantees that they will get continuing assistance in addition to individual sessions.

Creating a Network: Encouraging ties with other survivors promotes a feeling of community by allowing for the sharing of experiences and encouragement from one another.

➢ Proficiency in Culture

Cultural Sensitivity: It's critical to acknowledge and value the variety of survivors, including their varied cultural origins. The provision of individualized help is ensured by cultural competency.

Addressing Barriers: Removing cultural barriers makes services more accessible by fostering an environment that is inclusive and encouraging.

> **Specialized Approaches**

Evidence-Based Approaches: The special requirements of survivors can be catered for in trauma-specific treatments like EMDR, CBT, or DBT. Targeted and successful treatments are ensured by applying evidence-based strategies.

Holistic Integration: A holistic approach that addresses the psychological, cognitive, and physical components of the survivor's experience is made possible by integrating different therapy methods.

Raising Awareness

Raising awareness is a potent way to bring situations that require attention to light. Whether it is social, environmental, or health-related, the main objective of this chapter is to raise awareness about [particular issue].

> **Catalyzing Change**

Initiating Dialogue: Raising awareness acts as a catalyst for starting important conversations, which in turn catalyzes change. It asks people to talk about the relevant topics at hand as individuals, groups, and society.

Increasing Awareness: Increasing awareness frequently results in more robust advocacy campaigns. People are more inclined to support the cause and push for change when they are aware of how serious a situation is.

> ## Determining the intended audience

Tailoring Interaction: It's critical to recognize and comprehend the target audience to optimize effect. Making communications more relevant and interesting for target audiences guarantees that awareness campaigns are successful.

Using Diverse Channels: Awareness campaigns may reach a wider audience and be more easily accessible by utilizing a variety of communication channels, such as social media and community activities.

> ## Creating Narratives That Are Engaging

Humanizing the Issue: Telling personal tales makes the cause more relatable. Personal accounts foster empathy and a sense of connection, which helps a larger audience relate to the problem.

Showcasing impact: Emphasizing the influence in the actual world helps to reaffirm that each person's efforts, along with encouragement, may lead to good change.

> ### Making the Most of Technology: Digital Platforms

Campaigns on Social Media: Using social media to its full potential boosts awareness initiatives. Viral content, shareable images, and focused messages have the power to spread via digital media.

Interactive Websites: Establishing interactive websites or forums serves as a central location for community involvement, resources, and information.

> ### Working Together with Influencers: Empowering Voices

Influencer Collaborations: Working together with influencers, or those who have a lot of power and reach, may greatly increase awareness campaigns. Their support lends the cause legitimacy and publicity.

Celebrity Advocacy: Adding a high-profile element and drawing attention from a wider audience are the results of involving celebrities who are enthusiastic about the cause.

➤ Initiatives for Education

Including Awareness Themes in Curriculum: Including awareness themes in the school curriculum guarantees that the next generation is educated and prepared to participate in crucial conversations.

Youth Engagement: Giving students the freedom to spearhead awareness campaigns cultivates social consciousness and a feeling of accountability.

➤ Participation of the Community: Local Events

Setting Up Workshops: Organizing local events, workshops, or seminars helps the cause reach the community directly. Direct interaction and Q&A sessions are possible in these interactive forums.

Community Partnerships: Working together with nearby companies and groups fortifies links within the community and presents a unified face for awareness.

➤ Measuring Impact

Monitoring Engagement: Data and metrics are useful tools for gauging the effectiveness of awareness initiatives. Future tactics are informed by the analysis of audience input, engagement, and reach.

Feedback Loops: By establishing feedback channels, you may facilitate continuous communication with your audience and make necessary corrections and enhancements.

➢ Sustaining Momentum: Long-Term Strategies

Planning Strategically: The important thing is sustainability. Creating long-term plans guarantees that awareness campaigns will develop and stay pertinent over time.

Changing with the Times: Adaptability and flexibility are essential. Consciously adapting to shifting conditions and social dynamics guarantees the efficacy of awareness programs.

Prevention Strategies

Education and Consent

This chapter explores the crucial nexus between consent and education, highlighting the value of interactions that are courteous and well-informed. Fostering a culture of consent, encouraging healthy communication, and developing mutual respect all start with education.

> ### Comprehensive Sex Education's Fundamentals: Going Beyond Reproductive Health

Comprehensive Perception: The biological factors of reproduction are only one part of comprehensive sex education. It includes knowing healthy relationships, giving permission, communication skills, and emotional well-being.

Diverse and Inclusive: A comprehensive strategy promotes inclusion and makes sure that everyone is understood and valued by acknowledging a range of identities, orientations, and experiences.

> ### Commencing Early: Age-Appropriate Curriculum

Developmental Appropriateness: Information is adapted to each person's unique stage of cognitive and emotional development through age-appropriate education.

Creating Foundations: From infancy to adolescence, early intervention lays the groundwork for positive attitudes, effective communication, and a clear awareness of boundaries.

> ## Beyond a simple "yes" or "no,": Affirmative consent

Consent is defined as True consent that goes beyond a simple "yes" or "no." It is a passionate, continuing, and voluntary commitment to participate in any activity, acknowledging that each person is free to establish and modify their boundaries.

It's All About Communication: The foundation of consent is effective communication. A culture of consent is established by promoting candid communication, checking in with partners, and honoring limits.

> ## Establishing Boundaries

Self-Awareness: Before partaking in intimate activities, people should be conscious of who they are and what their boundaries are. People should be able to clearly explain their limitations thanks to education.

Respecting Boundaries: Consent education places a strong emphasis on the value of honoring the personal space of others and making sure that everyone is at ease.

> **Finding Expressions of Common Interest: Interpreting Nonverbal Cues**

Body Language: Recognizing nonverbal clues is essential to teaching consent. People must be taught how to read body language and identify cues that indicate discomfort or shared interest.

Teaching partners how to actively listen improves their capacity to detect both verbal and nonverbal signs, leading to a more profound comprehension of their goals and emotions.

> **Challenges and Nuances**

Complex Situations: Situations that include ambiguity and complexity should be covered in consent education. People require direction while negotiating unclear situations, realizing the value of ongoing communication, and honoring one another's emotions.

Substance Use and Consent: It's critical to discuss how substance use affects consent. It should be emphasized in education that poor judgment might make it difficult to offer willing and informed permission.

> **Digital Interactions**

Digital Age Consent: Online interactions are included in consent education. People need to understand how crucial it is to have an explicit, voluntary agreement in digital settings while also honoring personal space and limits.

Digital literacy: Encouraging digital literacy fosters a culture of consent in both the virtual and real worlds by assisting people in navigating online communication appropriately.

➤ Addressing Consent Violations

Encouraging Reporting: Consent education needs to provide people the confidence to report infractions without worrying about being judged. Developing resources and reporting systems that are encouraging guarantees that survivors get the help they require.

Community Accountability: Education ought to include a strong emphasis on how communities hold people accountable for their deeds, encouraging a group effort to establish safe places.

➤ Lifelong Learning

Continuous Dialogue: Learning consent is a lifetime process. Promoting constant communication, introspection, and knowledge of changing customs and traditions all help to create a culture that values consent.

Advocacy in Action: People who get consent education go on to promote change. Activism should be encouraged via education, pushing people to question social conventions and advance consent culture in larger settings.

Creating Safer Spaces

The idea of safer places transcends many domains, from real-world settings to virtual ones, encouraging an atmosphere in which everyone is valued and comfortable.

> **Inclusivity and Accessibility**

Universal Design: To ensure that people of all abilities can easily traverse and use the environment, physical environments should be built with universal accessibility in mind.

Accessible bathrooms, ramps, and sensory-friendly features are examples of inclusive facilities that are designed to accommodate a wide variety of demands.

> **Emergency Preparedness and Safety Procedures**

Open-Source Protocols: A commitment to the safety of everyone present in the area is communicated by establishing explicit safety procedures. People ought to be informed about safety precautions, evacuation routes, and emergency exits.

Frequent Safety Drills: By ensuring that residents are familiar with evacuation protocols, regular safety drills improve readiness for any emergencies.

> ### **Zero Tolerance for Discrimination and Harassment: Guidelines and Implementation**

All-encompassing Policies: Enforcing strict anti-discrimination and anti-harassment regulations promotes a secure atmosphere. These guidelines ought to be widely disseminated, freely available, and vigorously upheld.

Prompt action: Upholding the commitment to preserving a safe environment is reaffirmed by establishing systems for reporting and prompt action in incidents of harassment or discrimination.

> ### **Considering Mental Health**

Stigma Reduction: Promoting a culture that de-stigmatizes mental health helps people seek help without worrying about being judged.

Accessible Resources: Offering resources like mental health programs, counseling services, and stress-relieving areas improves residents' general well-being.

➢ **Cybersecurity Measures**

Data Protection: Protecting personal data and promoting trust in online environments are achieved by implementing strong cybersecurity measures.

Initiatives for Education: Raising user awareness of online safety, including how to identify and report cyber threats, contributes to the development of a safe online community.

➢ **Initiatives for Inclusivity and Diversity**

Reflecting Diversity: Ensuring that everyone feels seen and appreciated requires actively encouraging diversity in leadership, visual representation, and decision-making.

Inclusive programming: Creating activities and events that honor many identities, cultures, and viewpoints fosters a feeling of community.

➢ **Sensitivity Training**

Empathy and Understanding: Educating employees and community members about inclusion and sensitivity fosters an environment of empathy and understanding.

Conflict Resolution: By giving people the tools they need to resolve conflicts amicably, conflict may be avoided before it gets out of hand.

> **Bystander intervention and allies**

Bystander Intervention Training: Promoting bystander intervention training enables people to actively assist others and step in when there is a threat to their safety.

Allyship: Fostering allyship encourages people to speak up for the security and welfare of vulnerable groups, which helps to foster a culture of shared accountability.

> **Community Feedback and Continuous Improvement**

Feedback Systems: Creating avenues for community input guarantees that the area adapts to the shifting requirements and worries of its users.

Adaptive Strategies: Applying feedback to put adaptive strategies into practice shows a dedication to ongoing development and sensitivity to community dynamics.

Part 7: Moving Forward

Overcoming Challenges in the Healing Process

Addressing Societal Barriers

The goal of this chapter is to disentangle the complex network of social constraints impeding equality and progress. Individuals may make a positive impact on a society that is more inclusive and fair by being aware of, facing, and removing these barriers.

➢ Identifying Institutional Bias

Institutional Structures: The first step in removing these ingrained obstacles is recognizing the existence of systematic prejudice within institutions, laws, and practices.

Intersectionality: Adopting an intersectional perspective aids in identifying how various types of discrimination cross and impact people in different ways according to their distinct identities and experiences.

➢ Campaigning for Policy Changes

Policy Analysis: Making the case for changes to policies entails evaluating current ones to find instances of discrimination and suggesting changes that advance inclusion.

Community Mobilization: Organizing communities to support policy changes gives voices a greater platform and guarantees that the proposed changes take into account the needs and worries of the people who will be directly impacted.

> **Initiatives for Economic Empowerment**

Programs for Entrepreneurship: These initiatives offer pathways to economic empowerment by assisting underprivileged populations in starting and operating their businesses.

Equal Pay Advocacy: To alleviate economic inequities and eliminate gender-based wage discrepancies, advocacy for equal pay for equal labor is crucial.

> **Educational Equity and Access**

Equitable Resources: Reducing structural barriers that impede academic performance by making sure that educational opportunities, resources, and assistance are allocated fairly.

Varied Curriculum: A more thorough grasp of history and culture is promoted by implementing an inclusive, varied curriculum that takes into account the experiences and contributions of many cultures.

➢ Healthcare Access for All

Accessible Healthcare: Promoting inexpensive healthcare guarantees that all people, irrespective of financial situation, can obtain high-quality medical treatment.

Culturally Competent treatment: Encouraging cultural competence within the healthcare system helps to guarantee that patients from a variety of backgrounds receive courteous, efficient treatment while addressing inequities.

➢ Criminal Justice Reform

Sentencing Disparities: Racial and socioeconomic imbalances in the criminal justice system can be addressed by supporting impartial and equitable sentencing guidelines.

Focus on Rehabilitation: Putting less emphasis on punitive measures and more on rehabilitation encourages a more equal and just way to deal with crime and lower recidivism rates.

> **Dispelling Stereotypes and Media Representations**

Media Literacy: Promoting media literacy enables people to interact critically with and confront the preconceptions that the media perpetuates.

Encouraging Different Voices: Encouraging varied voices in media creation helps to provide inclusive and truthful depictions of a range of populations.

> **Building Bridges of Support**

Teaching Allies: Spreading awareness of the idea of allyship encourages the development of support systems across various populations and a feeling of unity.

Amplifying Marginalized Voices: To make sure that all viewpoints are acknowledged and heard, allies can utilize their privilege to raise the voices of oppressed populations.

> **Organizing Communities and Grassroots Movements**

Community Empowerment: Through community organizing and grassroots movements, people are given the ability to work together to overcome social obstacles and push for change from the bottom up.

Sustainable Activism: Establishing networks, promoting resilience, and making sure that initiatives have a long-lasting effect on social structures are all necessary to develop sustainable activist movements.

Promoting Long-Term Well-Being

➢ Holistic Health Procedures

Holistic Wellness: The cornerstone of holistic health is understanding the connections between one's physical, mental, and emotional well-being. Long-term well-being is enhanced by practices that take the full person into account.

Living Mindfully: Practicing mindfulness techniques like yoga, meditation, and deep breathing helps people become more aware of the present moment, which lowers stress and improves balance in general.

➢ Exercise and Dietary Practices

Balanced Nutrition: Making a healthy, balanced diet a priority gives the body the nutrition it needs to promote mental and emotional stability as well as physical health.

Frequent Exercise: Building the foundation for long-term well-being, frequent physical activity improves mood, lowers stress levels, and supports cardiovascular health.

> **Sustaining Mental Health**

Cultivating Resilience: Creating coping strategies, encouraging optimistic thinking, and accepting flexibility in the face of adversity are all part of developing emotional resilience.

Therapeutic Activities: Taking part in counseling or psychotherapy, for example, can help with stress management, mental health issues, and the promotion of general well-being.

> **Building Meaningful Relationships**

Relationships Are Important: Building deep bonds with loved ones, neighbors, and community members not only lowers feelings of loneliness but also offers emotional support and promotes long-term satisfaction.

Communication Skills: Gaining proficiency in communication enhances bonds between people and promotes empathy, understanding, and a feeling of community.

> **Work-Life Balance: Prioritizing Well-Being**

Healthy Boundaries: First Setting limits between one's personal and professional lives guarantees that people have time for leisure, relaxation, and happy, fulfilling pursuits.

Self-Care Routines: Including self-care activities in everyday schedules, such as taking pauses, engaging in hobbies, and getting enough sleep, promotes long-term well-being.

➢ Financial Literacy

Planning and Budgeting: Reducing stress and improving financial well-being are two benefits of developing financial literacy and implementing sound financial planning and budgeting techniques.

Emergency Preparedness: Setting up an emergency fund and making plans to improve financial security, offering stability and mental clarity.

➢ Lifelong Learning and Personal Development

Curiosity and Learning: Whether via formal schooling or self-directed inquiry, developing an inquisitive attitude and pursuing lifelong learning promotes human development and fulfillment.

Setting Objectives: Throughout a person's life, establishing significant objectives and benchmarks gives them a feeling of direction, inspiration, and success.

➢ Sustainable Living

Connection to Nature: Understanding the relationship between health and the environment helps people value sustainable living.

Minimizing Environmental Impact: Developing environmentally conscious behaviors, such as cutting back on waste and using resources wisely, benefits both individual and global well-being.

➢ Combining Joy and Leisure

Enjoyable Activities: Including leisure and enjoyment in daily life, whether via artistic endeavors, hobbies, or just spending time with loved ones, improves general well-being.

Developing Gratitude: Being grateful for life's little pleasures, connections, and achievements makes you happier and improves your well-being in the long run.

Conclusion

Looking Ahead: A Call to Action

The conclusion of this book acts as a rallying cry encouraging you to put the wisdom gained from previous chapters into action. It is an invitation to not only reflect on personal development but also to actively shape a future of positive transformation and collective well-being.

> **Reflecting on Personal Transformations**

Acknowledging Growth: Begin by expressing gratitude for personal transformations and reflecting on the lessons learned throughout the journey. Consider the strengths gained, challenges overcome, and the evolving sense of self.

Journaling Your Narrative: Encourage readers to keep a reflective journal, capturing moments of triumph, resilience, and personal growth. Documenting this narrative can serve as a powerful reminder of one's journey.

> ### Setting Intentional Goals: Vision for the Future

Clarifying Personal Values: Encourage readers to articulate their core values and aspirations. What kind of future do they envision for themselves and their communities?

SMART Goal Setting: Guide readers in setting Specific, Measurable, Achievable, Relevant, and Time-bound (SMART) goals. This structured approach helps translate aspirations into actionable steps.

> ### Cultivating a Growth Mindset

Embracing Challenges: Advocate for a growth mindset — the belief that abilities can be developed through dedication and hard work. Encourage a willingness to embrace challenges as opportunities for growth.

Lifelong Learning: Inspire readers to seek out learning opportunities continuously, whether through formal education, skill-building workshops, or exposure to diverse perspectives.

> ### Fostering Inclusivity and Community

Inclusive Practices: Call on readers to actively foster inclusivity within their communities. This includes embracing diversity, challenging biases, and creating spaces where everyone feels seen and heard.

Community Engagement: Encourage participation in community initiatives, whether through volunteer work, mentorship programs, or collaborative projects that address shared challenges.

> **Amplifying Voices**

Social Justice Advocacy: Motivate readers to become advocates for social change. This involves raising awareness about systemic issues, amplifying marginalized voices, and actively supporting initiatives that promote equity.

Participating in Movements: Inspire engagement in social justice movements, emphasizing that collective action is a potent force for driving societal transformations.

> **Environmental Stewardship**

Sustainable Practices: Call for environmental stewardship by adopting sustainable practices in daily life. This includes reducing waste, conserving resources, and supporting eco-friendly initiatives.

Advocating for Change: Encourage readers to advocate for policies and practices that promote environmental conservation, recognizing the interconnectedness of environmental well-being and human flourishing.

➤ Nurturing Healthy Relationships

Relationship Wellness: Emphasize the importance of cultivating healthy relationships built on communication, empathy, and mutual support. Healthy relationships contribute to personal well-being and the well-being of communities.

Conflict Resolution Skills: Provide guidance on developing effective conflict resolution skills, fostering resilience in relationships, and contributing to positive social dynamics.

➤ Empowering Minds

Supporting Educational Initiatives: Encourage readers to contribute to educational initiatives, whether through mentorship, scholarship programs, or advocacy for inclusive and accessible education.

Lifelong Learning Culture: Advocate for a culture of lifelong learning, recognizing education as a powerful tool for personal empowerment and societal progress.

➤ Harnessing Technology for Good

Responsible Tech Use: Acknowledge the role of technology in shaping the future and urge readers to use it responsibly. This includes promoting digital literacy, combating misinformation, and advocating for ethical tech practices.

Innovating for Social Impact: Inspire readers to explore ways in which technology can be harnessed for social impact, fostering innovations that address societal challenges.

> **Active Citizenship**

Voting and Civic Participation: Stress the importance of civic engagement, including voting in elections, participating in community forums, and staying informed about local and global issues.

Advocating for Change: Remind readers that active citizenship involves advocating for policies that align with values and contribute to the collective well-being.

> **Sharing Stories of Triumph**

Spreading Inspiration: Encourage readers to share their narratives of triumph and transformation. These stories serve as powerful tools for inspiring others and creating a ripple effect of positive change.

Digital Platforms and Community Building: Highlight the role of digital platforms in amplifying personal narratives and fostering online communities that support and uplift individuals on their journeys.

Resources for Survivors

From mental health support to legal assistance, the resources outlined here aim to serve as pillars of strength for those navigating the journey toward recovery.

➢ Mental Health and Counseling Services

Individual Counseling: Access to individual counseling services provides survivors with a safe space to explore and process their experiences, develop coping strategies, and work toward healing.

Group Therapy: Group therapy sessions offer a supportive community where survivors can connect with others who have shared experiences, fostering a sense of solidarity and understanding.

➢ Crisis Helplines and Hotlines

24/7 Hotlines: Crisis helplines provide immediate and confidential support for individuals in distress. Trained professionals are available to offer a listening ear, crisis intervention, and information on available resources.

Text and Online Chat Services: Some helplines offer text and online chat options, providing alternative means of communication for those who may find it challenging to speak over the phone.

> **Legal Support and Advocacy**

Legal Aid Organizations: Connect survivors with legal aid organizations specializing in issues related to sexual assault. These organizations can offer guidance on legal rights, assistance with protective orders, and support throughout legal proceedings.

Victim Advocates: Trained victim advocates can provide emotional support, accompany survivors to court, and help navigate the legal system, ensuring survivors feel empowered and informed.

> **Accessing Healthcare**

SANE Programs: Sexual Assault Nurse Examiner (SANE) programs provide specialized medical care and forensic exams for survivors. These programs prioritize survivors' comfort and consent throughout the examination process.

Sexual Health Clinics: Access to sexual health clinics ensures survivors receive comprehensive medical care, including testing for sexually transmitted infections and access to preventative measures.

Share Your Thoughts

Dear Esteemed Reader,

Thank you for embarking on the journey within the pages of "Psychology of Trauma Through Sexual Assault" Your engagement with this book is deeply appreciated, and your thoughts matter.

We invite you to share your feedback and leave a review to help us understand how this book has resonated with you. Your insights can contribute to fostering a supportive community for those navigating their paths of triumph and transformation.

To leave your feedback and review:

- Scan the QR code provided below with your smartphone's camera app or a QR code scanner app.

- Once scanned, you'll be directed to the author's page.

- Scroll down to find the section for leaving a review.

Your feedback is invaluable, and we look forward to hearing your thoughts. As a token of appreciation, take a moment to explore the author's page for additional works that may pique your interest. Your support means the world to us.

Thank you for being a part of this community of readers and for sharing in the journey of empowerment and resilience.

With gratitude,

Flawless Dave